MANAGING YOUR CREDIT REPORT
LIKE YOUR BANK ACCOUNT

MANAGING YOUR CREDIT REPORT
LIKE YOUR BANK ACCOUNT
Second Edition

INCLUDES TIPS ON GETTING OUT OF DEBT

SHERMAN FOWLER

This printing published by Prestige Enterprises Books
San Clemente, California, 92674

For
Janet Fowler
"The wind beneath my wings"

Published by Prestige Enterprises Books, P.O. Box 5736, San Clemente, CA 92674

Cover Design: Fowler Design Group

Printed in the United States of America

Library of Congress Control Number: 2015930401

Fowler, Sherman
    Managing your credit report like your bank account / Sherman Fowler

Includes bibliographical references and index
                ISBN 9780988925502

January 2010 First Edition
January 2015 Second Edition

Revision History for the Second Edition:

January 2010 First Printing
January 2015 Second Printing

IMPORTANT - READ THIS BEFORE GETTING STARTED

This document was created as a conduit of information and should in no way be used or substituted for legal advice. If you feel that you need legal assistance, talk to, or hire, a professional lawyer to assist you with any legal matters that you may have.

The information contained in this book is to help educate and inform the consumer from an overview perspective of credit related subject matters and to give ideas on how to become more aware of issues like identity theft protection. This will enable you, the consumer, to become more aware of the importance of recognizing the value of credit and the importance of credit management.

ACKNOWLEDGMENT

I would like to express my gratitude to the many people who saw me through this book. To all those who provided support, talked things over, read, wrote, and offered comments.

Above all I would like to thank my wife, Janet and the rest of my family, who supported and encouraged me in spite of all the time it took me away from them. It was a long and difficult journey for them.

I would like to thank Navideh Mostajab, Darius Vasefi, and Jim Miklich for helping me with the editing, proofreading, and their encouragement to complete this book.

TABLE OF CONTENTS

Foreword

When I met Sherman Fowler in 2000, it was in his capacity as an IT Network Manager for a large real estate company. Over time I found out that he had been compiling the information contained in the first edition of "Managing Your Credit Like Your Bank Account".

Later our careers moved us into the development of automated underwriting systems where we created data interfaces between credit reporting agencies and lenders. A few years ago, Sherman authored a class for broker training on re-issued reports, merging of conflicting data, and rapid corrections. This was needed due to often erroneous data on many people's credit reports, and resulted in many lost loan closings because of common data problems endemic to the credit reporting industry.

Sherman has a passion for helping people, and this was evident as he would encounter one person after another who had always worked hard, saved up and were ready to buy their first house, but had been denied a loan due to their credit score. Patiently, but with systematic enthusiasm, he would show them where to get their reports, how to locate errors or inaccurate information - and how to document the dispute. Over the course of several months, all the legitimate errors would be corrected, and they would finally be able to get the right loan. Interest in the book began to pick up as people started giving it careful attention.

The second edition of "Managing Your Credit Like Your Bank Account" contains precise and accurate information that you will find useful even if you have a perfect credit file. Ask anyone who has been the victim of identity theft how easy it was to deal with the fallout from that. The information on how to both protect yourself, and repair the damage is contained in this book.

Sherman's background in project management has given him a very organized approach, and he has provided an instruction manual on how to improve your credit score in a systematic way that anyone should be able to understand.

Rick Bellows
MBA, PMP

Preface

Do you know what affects your credit rating? One of every five American consumers has errors on his or her credit report. Understanding your Credit Report can help you clean up your credit and increase your credit score.

This book was written to empower anyone that would like to clean up their credit, increase their credit score and have favorable credit when applying for a loan, credit card or employment.

"Managing Your Credit Report Like Your Bank Account" is a time saver when it comes to understanding the process of cleaning up your credit. You could spend hours, days, months, or maybe years trying to find all the information you need to clean up and improve your credit to get a higher credit score.

The information you need to improve your credit score and clean up your credit is now all right here in one place in this amazing book. Inside this powerful book is a systematic step by step credit clean up and credit improvement system that really works!

When you read this book you will gain the power and the knowledge to clean up and improve your credit. Also, you will learn what the credit reporting agencies don't want you to know when it comes to cleaning up and improving your credit to increase your credit score.

Inside this book are tips that will guide you toward cleaning up your credit and improving your credit score. You will gain valuable knowledge on how to better understand your credit report and how to manage your credit. Included in this book are important tips on managing the factors that affect your credit rating like debt ratio, the percent of your credit that you are utilizing.

Now you can save thousands of dollars and countless hours of searching for information to clean up and improve your credit score. This systematic approach to improving and cleaning up credit is simple to follow and very easy to understand.

I want to thank everyone who encouraged me to write this book to help those that would like to know how to clean up their credit and improve their credit score.

Let "Managing Your Credit Report Like Your Bank Account" *show you how!*

Credit and money go hand in hand and this book is designed to serve as a guide to those that want to be impowered with the knowledge to clean up their credit, improve their credit score, and manage their credit.

INTRODUCTION

Welcome and congratulations on taking the first step toward cleaning up your credit, managing your credit and improving your credit score.

I would first like to say that *"We only repair things that are broken or things that are in need of repair. Your credit is not broken nor in need of being repaired"*. Credit is a money management issue that needs to be managed not repaired.

What does managing your credit report like your bank account mean? Credit management is the act of changing one's thinking about how they view their credit worthiness and understanding the importance of having the right information when it comes to cleaning up your credit, increasing your credit score, and managing your credit.

How would you feel if you did not receive your bank statement about your money from the bank every month? You would be concerned, and a little scared maybe? You would contact the bank right away to see why you have not received your monthly bank statement.

Your bank will issue a statement each month to you and when it arrives you pick it up and look over everything very carefully. When you notice a mistake or an error you call the bank to make sure the bank is taking the proper actions to make the necessary corrections to your account.

When cleaning up your credit and improving your credit score, take the same approach when reviewing your credit report. If you find errors on your credit report, take action to make the necessary corrections.

If you ever wanted to know how to improve your credit score, use the information provided here to clean up your credit, and save thousands of dollars in the process.

Read through the material in this book and you will acquire the knowledge needed to clean up your credit and the power to implement that knowledge to achieve your goal of cleaning up your credit to have a higher credit score.

Let "Managing Your Credit Report Like Your Bank Account" show you how!

CHAPTER 1

GETTING STARTED WITH THE CREDIT MANAGEMENT PROCESS

We start by looking at the credit management process to understand how it works and why it is important to change your thinking about credit. As you read through this material, think of your credit as a valuable form of money that needs to be managed and not repaired.

The importance of understanding that your credit is a valuable resource, or a form of money that should be managed, will be of great value as you continue your efforts to clean up your credit and achieve a higher credit score.

Improving your credit and achieving a higher credit score starts with understanding how the credit management process works. In this chapter we will look at the credit management process and how it works.

The graphic below shows the credit management process.

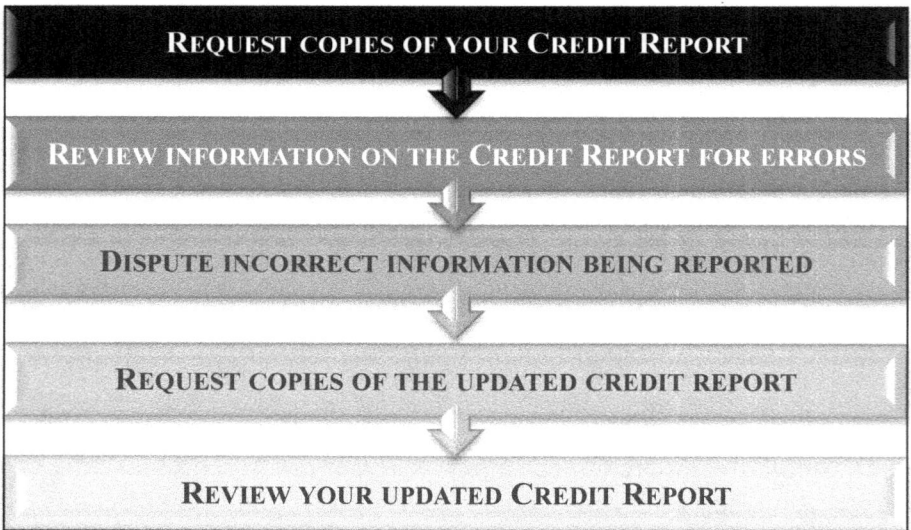

We will take a closer look at the credit management process in more detail as you continue to read through the material in the following chapters.

THE CREDIT MANAGEMENT PROCESS OVERVIEW

You should request copies of your credit report from the (3) three major credit reporting bureaus. Remember if you are married, request copies of your credit report separately for both you and your spouse.

Review all of the following information on the credit report

Your name, address, social security number, date of birth, former address, public records, and inquiries.

Check for **typos** and **inaccuracies** on your credit report. If any of your personal information is incorrect for any reason, it will cause an alert on your credit report. Alerts appear on your credit report as **Checkpoints**, **AKA**, and or a **Hawk alert**.

Most mortgage companies use your **social security number**, your **first name**, **middle name**, and **last name** to identify an individual when requesting a copy of your credit report. So double check to make sure your personal information is being reported correctly.

When writing your dispute letter or using the internet to dispute account information, **include all the line items that you want removed** from your credit report. It is very important that you include all the accounts at the same time when you send your dispute letter via certified mail with return receipt requested. This is the time to list everything that you disagree with on your credit report.

After receiving your return receipt back in the mail, *(to show proof that you did send the letter by certified mail)* confirm that the credit reporting bureaus have received your letter *(this means making a phone call to the three credit reporting bureau)* and ask the person on the phone *(be sure to ask for their name)* "has the investigation begun?" More on dispute letters in chapter 10.

Remember your reason for wanting to know this information. You want to start keeping track of their progress in investigating your credit report information. The reporting agencies have 30 days to correct your credit report and send you an updated copy of your report. This overview of the credit management process illustrates some very important steps to take towards improving your credit and achieving a higher FICO score.

CHAPTER 2

HOW DOES CREDIT REPORTING WORK?

As consumers we are accustomed to being able to buy things that we want by leveraging them. That is, we sign our name and some company guarantees the payment on our behalf. That company is called a creditor and it relies on another type of company called a credit bureau to decide whether or not to extend credit to you.

Credit bureaus are companies that make their living receiving information about our financial habits and then selling that information to others who are considering extending credit to us. It's important to remember that these credit-reporting companies are not divisions of the government. They are just a business like any other and must abide by the rules, regulations and laws established by Congress. Most Americans think that these companies are the government and are therefore afraid to confront them when they make unfair character references about us.

Before you attempt to enhance your credit to a favorable standing, there are some important facts you should be aware of. Millions of people today are in the same predicament as you are and want to improve their credit to a more favorable standing.

The Federal Trade Commission (FTC) reported that some 40 million Americans have a mistake on their credit report, and 10 million are potentially denied credit, or paying a higher interest rate as a result. These are eye-opening numbers.

The good news is that it is possible to remove negative items from your credit report legally without paying thousands of your hard earn dollars to a "credit repair" company. The information contained in this book will help you to clean up your credit and increase your credit score.

CHAPTER 3

WHO ARE THE CREDIT REPORTING AGENCIES?

The three big reporting agencies in the United States which can affect your buying power when it comes to using your credit score are; **Experian**, **Equifax**, and **TransUnion**. These are three different companies, and again they are not a government agency. They are simply companies that serve as a data warehouse.

These credit reporting agencies are also referred to as "Credit Bureaus", and are central repositories of integrated data they compile from your credit information. Your credit information is collected from creditors that report your credit information to the bureaus. That information is sold to companies who will use it to market to you if they find that you would be a potential customer for a credit card. It is used when you apply for employment, applying for a loan, or any legitimate business need.

The FTC released a report that found that 21 percent of a representative group of American consumers discovered a "confirmed material error" in at least one of the credit reports issued by the big three credit reporting bureaus.

Your information on file at these credit bureaus includes:
• Your consumer identification information such as full name, address, employment, spouses name and employer.
• Your Credit history including: account numbers, date initiated, amount borrowed, terms, and type of credit, along with the number of payments outstanding balances, amounts past due and the frequency of lateness.
• Derogatory information like public records such as law suits, judgments, tax liens, or bankruptcies.
• Inquiries of companies or individuals who have requested a copy of your credit report within the past 18 months

Data is added to existing information on your credit file every month that gets compiled to make up your credit history. Businesses can then decide your credit worthiness based on this data that is added to your credit file.

DO YOU KNOW WHAT'S IN A FICO SCORE?

The credit data used to calculate your FICO Score comes from (5) five categories. Reflected in the chart below is the percentage value of each category used in calculating your FICO Score.

This chart shows the FICO Score break down

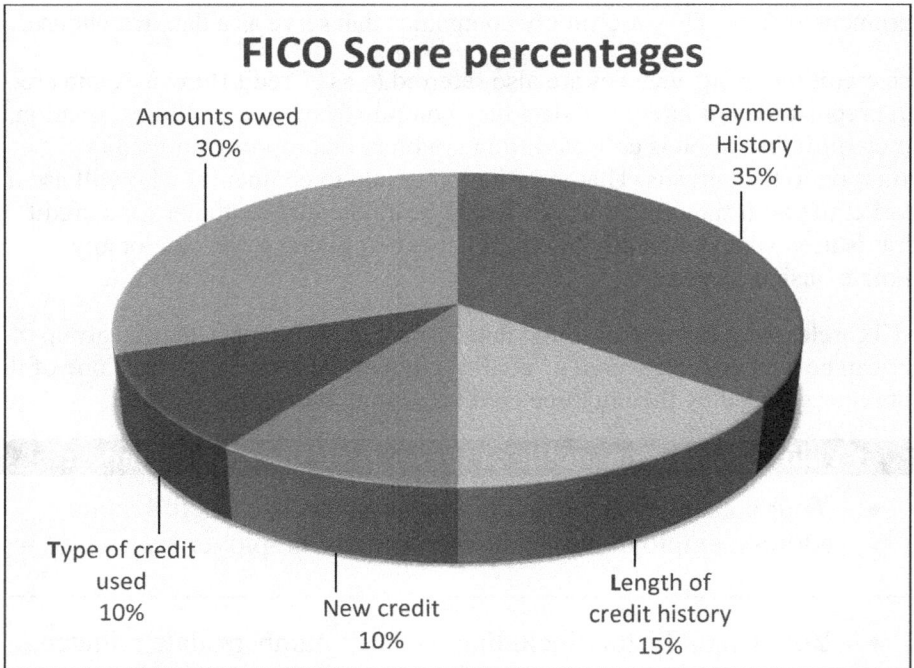

FICO Score percentages

Amounts owed 30%

Payment History 35%

Type of credit used 10%

New credit 10%

Length of credit history 15%

Now that you know the five categories and their percentage value used to calculate your FICO Score. You can see the importance of paying your bills on time to increase your FICO Score. Paying your bills late will cause you to have a lower FICO Score.

The **Fair Credit Reporting Act** or **FCRA** is enforced by the **Federal Trade Commission** or **FTC**. The purpose of the FCRA is to insure accuracy and privacy of the information used in consumer credit reports. Recent amendments expand your rights and place additional requirements on your information and how it is used. Any company that supplies information about you to credit reporting agencies and those that use consumer reports must abide by these rules. If you have a complaint about these businesses you can file it with the Federal Trade Commission.

WHAT'S YOUR FICO SCORE? (720-850, 650-700, 620-650, 600)

Your FICO score is a measure of your ability to make payments on time and manage your credit. It helps lenders determine how likely you are to pay back your loan. The number is calculated using a formula created by Fair Isaac Corporation, which is why it's also referred to as your FICO score.
Let's look at what these numbers mean and what they will do for you, the consumer, financially.

CREDIT RATINGS - EXCELLENT, MODERATE, BAD, VERY BAD

720 and above - You have excellent credit and will qualify for some of the best programs offered by lenders. It shows that your accounts are paid on time with no negative public records and you are an excellent credit risk.

650 to 700 - You have moderate credit and will not qualify for the best programs offered by lenders. These scores show that you may have high credit card debt, may have applied for too many new credit cards and are a moderate credit risk that qualifies you for decent rates.

620 to 650 - You have bad credit and will not qualify for the best programs offered by lenders. You have high amounts of credit card debt, may have late payments, may have collections, and bankruptcy records. To lenders you are a high credit risk and may be difficult to be approved for a standard credit option.

Below 600 - You have very bad credit and are a very high credit risk, very high credit debt, apply for too many new credit accounts, late payments, collection accounts and it will be very difficult to get approved for a loan or new credit without having a co-signer work with you. This will also require you to make a large down payment when applying for new credit.

Having poor credit may even hamper your job search. While a company interviewing you is not permitted to access your score, they are allowed to request (with your written consent) a modified version of your credit report to see whether you have a history of meeting your financial responsibilities. Potential landlords may also access your credit report before you sign a lease.

7

CHAPTER 4

HOW LONG IS CREDIT INFORMATION RETAINED?

To understand how long an item is reported on your credit report, let's take a look at how long an item can remain on a credit report.

THIS TABLE SHOWS HOW LONG ITEMS WILL REMAIN ON YOUR CREDIT FILE	
Accounts paid as agreed	As a rule will remain for years.
Accounts not paid as agreed	As a rule will remain for **(7) seven years.**
Bankruptcy information	May be reported for **(10) ten years** from the date filed.
Bankruptcy under chapter 7, chapter 11 or, a non-discharged or, dismissed years from the date filed.	As a rule will remain on your credit report for **(10) ten years** from the date filed.
Discharged chapter 13 bankruptcy	As a rule will remain on your credit report for **(7) seven years.**
Inquires	Can remain on your credit report for up to **(2) two years** or until you request that they be removed if the inquires were not a valid offer for credit.
Judgments	As a rule will remain on your credit report for **(7) seven years** from the date filed.
Late – payment history	As a rule will remain for **(7) seven years.**
Revolving debt with late payments history	As a rule will remain for **(7) seven years.**
Student loans	As a rule will remain on your credit report until **paid in full**.
Tax liens	As a rule will remain on your credit report for **(7) seven years** from the date filed or date paid in full.
Unpaid tax liens	As a rule will remain on your credit report until **paid in full**.

Most credit information stays on your report for (7) seven years.

CHAPTER 5

THE (4) FOUR WAYS TO OBTAIN COPIES OF YOUR CREDIT REPORT

US MAIL

In person

Internet

Telephone landline

METHODS OF OBTAINING COPIES OF YOUR CREDIT REPORT

Obtaining copies of your credit report is something that each and every one of us should do at least once a year to know what is being reported about us.
Here are the (4) four ways to obtain a copies of your credit report.

In Person

Obtain a copy of your credit report by appearing in person and requesting a copy.

Request by phone

Obtain a copy over the phone by calling Experian, Equifax, and TransUnion to request a copy of your credit report.

Internet

If you have a computer, smart phone, mobile device and access to the Internet you can obtain a copy of your credit reports by going online to one of the following links:

www.experian.com
www.equifax.com
www.transunion.com

United States Postal Service

A copy may also be obtained by mail if you send the proper identification along with your request for a copy of your report.
Forms of identification should be a copy of your **social security card** along with a copy of a **utility** or **phone bill** to assist in identifying you and your current address.

Authorization Letter

You can have someone else obtain a copy of your report if you provide a letter authorizing the bureau to release a copy of your report to that person.

You should order a copy of your credit report from all three of the above credit reporting agencies. If you are married, order credit reports for the both of you. **If you have children order a copy of their report too. Due to identity thief you want to keep your children's identity and social security numbers safe.**

OBTAINING FREE COPIES OF YOUR CREDIT REPORTS

You may obtain a FREE copy of your credit report for the following reasons
If you have been **denied credit** because of a credit report generated by any reporting bureau. Contact the bureau that reported the information and have them send you a copy of your report for **FREE**.
If adverse information is being reported on your credit report and you are made aware that this is happening, you have a right to ask that the reporting bureau provide you with a free copy of your report.
(FACTA) – The Fair and Accurate Credit Transactions Act also entitles all consumers to a free annual credit report to verify all information on your report is accurate.
For example, when a company sends you a letter inquiring about money you owe or calls you to inquire about a debt. You have been made aware of the information being reported.

You are entitled to a **free** copy of your credit report under Federal law.

When requesting a copy of your credit report using one of the (4) four methods discussed earlier. You will need to provide the following information;

- Include **your birth name** (The name given to you on your birth certificate) *No nick names.*
- Your current **mailing address.**
- **Social Security** number.
- Make a copy of your social security card and include it with your letter.
- Include your **date of birth.**
- Make a copy of a utility bill and include with your letter.

A copy of the utility bill will help them know that they are sending the report to the right person that requested the report.

If you are sending your request by US Mail, send it as certified mail.

Note:

Never send a copy of your driver's license or a copy of anything that you do not want on your credit report. If you do, that information will be placed on your report and sold.

Send a copy of your certified letter to all three addresses below:		
Experian Consumer Relations **P.O. Box 2002** **Allen, TX 75013-2104**	**Equifax Consumer Relations** **P.O. Box 740241** **Atlanta, GA 30374-0193**	**TransUnion Consumer Relations** **P.O. Box 1000** **Chester, PA 19022**
www.Experian.com **888-397-3742**	**www.equifax.com** **800-685-1111**	**www.TransUnion.com** **800-888-1000**

The current addresses for Experian, Equifax & TransUnion at the time this book was printed.

The cost for a credit report will vary per state. You can order a free copy of your credit report once a year. In your request letter that you send to Equifax and Trans Union, state that you were referred by Experian and they will send you a free credit report

CERTIFIED MAIL AND RECORD KEEPING

Always send certified mail to these reporting bureaus when you mail your letters to them if you are using US Mail. It helps to start a paper trail and will be useful as you continue to work on cleaning up your credit report so you can begin to manage your credit report like your bank account.

Also, by sending certified mail they have to have someone from their company sign for the letter. Now they can't say that they never received your letter because you sent it by certified mail.

When using the internet to request a copy of your report it might be a good idea to print out any web page that records the online transaction. The web page that you make prints of will contain the date and time of your online request and will become part of your records.

CHAPTER 6

HOW TO INTERPRET A CREDIT REPORT

INTERPRETING YOUR CREDIT REPORT

Once you've obtained a copy of your credit report, you will see what your creditors are saying about you. However, credit reports can be a little confusing.

The sample credit report below shows the different sections that are included on a credit report.

PERSONAL INFORMATION SECTION			
Jane Doe 456 Your Street Your Town, State	(Date of report) Date __ / __ / __	SSN.123-45-6789 D.O.B.__/__/__	Credit Service Assoc Business address City, State, Zip Phone Number

Company Name	Acct: Number	Whose Account	Date Opened	Months Reviewed	Date of Last Activity	High Credit	Terms	Bal. Past Due Status-Date Due
Sam's Bank 2400	3445920930	I	10/00	28	09/03	740	36	R1
K-Mart 1200	2323414121	J	07/04	36	10/05	760	24	R1
The Bank 1000	M23987823	M	09/05	48	04/0_	790	_	I9

CREDIT HISTORY SECTION

PROR PAYING HISTORY- 30 (03) 60 (04) 9_____ -------- _/2000-R1 04/2001-R1 07/2002-R3
- COLLECTION REPORTED 9/00: ASSIGNED ON 10/00 TO GET THEM COLLECTION
- COMPANY (000) 000-0000
- CLIENT: LAWER PEN HEAD THOMAS, AMOUNT $__00 UNPAID 10/00
- ACOUNT NUMBER 456__8

PUBLIC RECORDS AND ADDITIONAL INFORMATION

- TAX LEN FILED 6/00. LOS ANGELES I.D. #9004-ABC: PLAINTIFF PLANET EARTH, AMOUNT $_____00

- LIEN FIELD 9/01: LOS ANGELES, AMOUNT $25000.00, OPTION ONE MORTGAGE, RELEASED 07/05

ADDITIONAL INFORMATION

- FORMER ADDRESS 934 FRONT STREET, SEAL BEACH, CA 90034
- FORMER ADDRESS 4920 MILLER DANA POINT, CA 39023

COMPANIES THAT REQUESTED YOUR CREDIT HISTORY		
03/05/00	CARS ARE US	05/09/00
05/30/03	K-MART	09/01/04
09/03/06	CAPITAL ONE	07/04/00

PERSONAL IDENTIFIERS

I. D. SECTION - CONTAINS IDENTIFYING INFORMATION	
Your Birth Name	The name that is associated with your social security number and printed on your birth certificate.
Mailing address History	This section will display history information about where you have lived. Like your current address, your last address, your addresses in the past.
Social Security Number	Your SSN is found in this section.
Date of Birth / D.O.B.	Your D.O.B. is found in this section
Spouse's Name *(if applicable)*	The name of your spouse will be displayed in this section of the credit report.

Take your time when reviewing the **I.D.** information to make sure all the entries are correct. One bad piece of information and the credit history listed on your report could be wrong.

CHAPTER 7

THE CREDIT HISTORY SECTION

The history section of the report contains a list of your open and paid credit accounts and indicates any late payments reported by your creditors. Although it may seem a little tedious, it's essential that you read through this section very thoroughly. If you find any information that is incorrect or accounts that don't belong to you, you'll need to submit a dispute letter to the credit-reporting agency or go online to the credit-reporting agencies website to dispute any wrong information on your credit report.

THE BASIC FORMAT FOR THE CREDIT HISTORY SECTION	
Company Name	Identifies the company that is reporting the information.
Account Number	Lists your account number with the company.
Whose Account	Indicates who is responsible for the account and the type of participation you have with the account. Abbreviations may vary depending on the reporting agency but here are some of the most common:

ABBREVIATIONS	
I	Individual
U	Undesignated
J	Joint
A	Authorized User
M	Maker
T	Terminated
C	Co-maker/Co-signer
S	Shared

Date Opened	This is the month and year you opened the account with the credit grantor.
Months Reviewed	Lists the number of months the account history has been reported.
Last Activity	Indicates the date of the last activity on the account. This may be the date of your last payment or last charge.
Reviewed	Shows number of months reviewed.
High Credit	Represents the highest amount charged or the credit limit. If the account is an installment loan, the original loan amount will be listed.
Terms	For installment loans, the number of installments may be listed or the amount of the monthly payments. For revolving accounts, this column is often left blank.
Balance	Indicates the amount owed on the account at the time it was reported.
Past Due	This column lists any amount past due at the time the information was reported.
Status	A combination of letters and numbers are used to indicate the type of account and the timeliness of payment.
Date Reported	Indicates the last time information on this account was updated by your creditor

ABBREVIATIONS FOR THE TYPE OF ACCOUNTS

(O) – Open	(R) – Revolving	(I) - Installment

An abbreviation for Timeliness of Payment varies among agencies.
Numbers are used to represent how current you are in your payments. Current or "paid as agreed" is usually represented by 0 or 1. Larger numbers (up to 9) indicate that an account is past due.

CHAPTER 8

COURTHOUSE RECORDS

This section may also be referred to as Public Records. Here you'll find a listing of public record items (obtained from local, state and federal courts) that reflect your history of meeting financial obligations.

PUBLIC RECORDS INFORMATION	
BANKRUPTCY RECORDS	Bankruptcy records are reported.
TAX LIENS	All tax liens will be reported
JUDGMENTS	Recorded judgments are reported.
COLLECTION ACCOUNTS	Collection information is reported.
OVERDUE CHILD SUPPORT *(IN SOME STATES)*	Delinquent child support data is reported.

Look closely at all the information listed. If anything is mistaken, contact the credit bureau and submit a dispute letter.

In today's high tech world, you can go to the three credit bureau's websites to dispute incorrect information on your credit report.

ADDITIONAL INFORMATION
This section consists primarily of former addresses and past employers as reported by your creditors.

FILING FOR BANKRUPTCY

In October of 2005 requirements for filing for bankruptcy changed. The **Bankruptcy Abuse Prevention and Consumer Protection Act (BAPCPA)** of 2005 substantially revised the rules and qualifications for bankruptcy. You will need a lawyer to advise you of your rights under this new bankruptcy law and to help you understand the new requirements for filing a bankruptcy.

Despite these major changes to the bankruptcy laws, the **federal government's expectations are that approximately 80 percent of those filing bankruptcy will remain eligible for chapter 7 bankruptcies**. This is the kind of bankruptcy where you do not have to pay your unsecured creditors. An **unsecured creditor** is a creditor other than a preferential creditor that does not have the benefit of any security interests in the assets of the debtor.

The total number of cases filed under the old bankruptcy laws that expired in October of 2005 was much greater than the supporters of the new bankruptcy laws anticipated.

COLLECTION ACCOUNTS SECTION

Accounts that have been referred to collection agencies in the last (7) seven years will be reported in this section of the credit report. The name of the collection agency will be listed along with the amount you owe and, in some cases, their contact information. If a collection is listed on your report that does not look familiar to you, contact the credit bureau and submit a dispute letter.

For your own peace of mind, you may also want to contact the collection agency to determine the nature of the account. Here are a few reasons why;

You may find out that the collection account is NOT yours.

Perhaps it belongs to someone whose name or social security number is very similar to yours. If this is the case, ask the collection agency to acknowledge this fact in writing. They should send a copy of the letter to you **AND** the credit reporting agency so that the mistaken information can be cleared from your report.

You may find out that the collection account IS yours.

If so, it is in your best interest to determine the accuracy of the amount of the collection account and make arrangements to satisfy your obligation as quickly as possible. Once the collection account has been paid, you should request a letter from the collection agency to this effect. Again, make sure the credit reporting agency gets a copy of the letter so that they can list the account as paid.

CHAPTER 9

INQUIRY SECTION

This section contains a list of the businesses that have received your credit report in the last 24 months. If you find the names of businesses that sound unfamiliar, you should find out who they are and why they're looking at your credit file! The credit-reporting agency may be able to help you with contact information.

Authorization • Inquires • Legitimate Business Need Selling information
● Remember, only companies that have received your written authorization should be able to check your credit history.
● Too many inquiries can prevent you from having the credit score you want and obtaining your financial goals you deserve.
● Companies are allowed to pull your credit because of the *"Legitimate business need"* clause in the law. These types of inquiries are called **prescreening inquiries**.
● Remember, credit reporting bureaus are in the business of selling your information and they charge a fee for membership. They also charge you a fee for your own information.

A company will also look at your credit report to see if you would be a good candidate to market their product to. If a company or multiple companies do this multiple times within an unacceptable period of time, it will become a negative on your report until you dispute the inquiry and request to have it removed from your credit report. When multiple companies are doing this on a daily basis to your credit report, the inquiries begin to add up. If you are a homeowner you will want to really manage the number of inquires that appear on your credit report. Include all inquires in your dispute letter the first time. You want to dispute everything at once.

HOW TO DISPUTE INFORMATION ON YOUR CREDIT REPORT?

When starting the process of disputing line items on your credit report it is very important to remember that this is a *process*. Track your progress by making notes and creating a folder to house all of your documents relating to your credit report enhancement process.

WHAT YOU NEED TO KNOW TO START THE DISPUTE PROCESS

If you are not using the internet to dispute accounts on your credit report and choose instead to write letters, keep this in mind. To get a quick response to your request, your letters should be **hand written on notebook paper and not typed**. You want your dispute letter to stand out from all of the thousands of typed dispute letters that arrive at the bureau's office every day.

Include all of the line items that you wish to dispute at the same time when you write your dispute letter. Trying to address line items two and three at a time will cause delays in cleaning up your credit report and extend the time for the credit bureaus to investigate your dispute. Also, you do not want the bureaus to think that you are using a credit repair company. If the credit bureaus think that you are using a credit repair company it could cause delays in the process. Remember this is a process that will take 30 to 45 days to complete.

To keep track of this process you will want to create a paper trail. Sending your letter using certified mail *only* with a Domestic Return Receipt request, helps create the desired paper trail. The United States Postal service calls this their PS Form 3811 and can be picked up at any post office for **FREE**.

THREE THINGS TO FOCUS ON IN YOUR DISPUTE LETTER	
Items that are inaccurate	Dispute information not being reported correctly.
Items that are non-verifiable	Dispute information that has not been proven to be true.
Items that are beyond the statute of limitations	Dispute information where the statute of limitations has passed, but is still being reported.

Remember to keep your dispute letter brief and to the point. You do not want your letter to be rejected because the credit bureaus think that you are using a credit repair company.

USING THE SAMPLE LETTERS

Located in this book are sample letters for you to use as a guide in your credit improvement process. Take a look at the sample letters and choose the right one for your scenario.

CHOOSING THE CORRECT SAMPLE LETTER

Example - 1

- If the account is old, you will want to choose the sample letter **"beyond the statute of limitations"**.

Example - 2

- If the accounts listed are not yours, choose the sample letter for **"information that does not belong to you"**.

NOTE:

Remember if you are not using the internet to dispute and correct the information that is being reported on your credit report, hand write your dispute letter; do not type your dispute letter.

Be sure to sign and date all letters. Include; **your name**, **social security number**, **date of birth**, and your **mailing address**. After you receive the returned receipt from the three credit bureaus follow up with a phone call to confirm that your letter was received and to start the clock ticking on the 30 days that the bureaus have to investigate your dispute.

ONLINE DISPUTE

If you choose to dispute online, you should know that many online dispute forms contain arbitration clauses which can affect your consumer rights. The credit bureaus bury waiver clauses in the click agreement, so, by clicking, "I Accept," you're giving up the right to sue them if they do something wrong or if they continue to fail to remove errors that are on your credit report. You are giving up your right to sue them and your claim would have to be resolved by a single arbitrator and not by the courts. Arbitration hearings are less consumer-friendly than traditional court trials, and potentially less fair.

Getting the process started

So your objective is to get the bureaus started on your dispute letter as soon as the bureau receives your letter. Again, make a phone call to confirm that the credit bureaus have received your letter after the return receipt form is mailed back to you. This will push buttons in the investigation process of your dispute letter. That's why you want to get the bureaus attention the first time around when sending your dispute letter.

You do not want them to think your claim is a questionable claim. If they misinterpret your claim, they will mail you a letter stating that your claim is "Frivolous and Irrelevant".

LETTER WRITING TIPS

- When writing your dispute letter be sure to give a reason why you are disputing the inaccuracy on your credit report.

- Avoid writing down details of the dispute like **it's not your account** because the name on the account is spelled incorrectly. Use a generalized approach when writing your letter.

NEVER! Attempt to correct personal information until all of the negatives have been removed.

NOTE
Anything that you don't want to appear on your credit report should not be included in your dispute letter.

When communicating with the bureaus the words you choose are very important in getting their attention. This is where semantics enters into play. Choose words like the following:

CHOOSING THE RIGHT WORDS	
Paid	This account was paid off.
In Full	This account was paid in full.
Promptly	I paid this account and was never late.

Stay away from saying that an account was late or wasn't late. Say something more to the effect of the account was **never** late. Remember you are disputing accounts on your credit report and would like an investigation of your disputes. Now it's up to the bureaus to investigate your disputes and do the work of verifying that your data is being reported correctly or incorrectly.

CHAPTER 10

DISPUTE
SAMPLE LETTER
SECTION

ITEMS THAT DO NOT BELONG TO YOU

BUREAU NAME   YOUR NAME
ADDRESS   ADDRESS
CITY, ST, ZIP   CITY, ST, ZIP
CUSTOMER REL   SS#,   D.O.B.

To whom it may concern,

The following items appearing on my credit report do not belong to me. These accounts must have been placed on my credit report in error. Please investigate and delete these items in order to reflect a true and accurate picture of my credit history.

Co Name:

1)

2)

3)

4)

5)

I'll wait 30 days from the date you receive this letter for you to complete the investigation.

Sincerely,

ITEMS BEYOND THE STATUTE OF LIMITATIONS

BUREAU NAME   YOUR NAME
ADDRESS   ADDRESS
CITY, ST, ZIP   CITY, ST, ZIP
CUSTOMER REL.   SS#, D.O.B.

To whom it may concern,

The following items listed on my credit report are being reported beyond the statute of limitations. These accounts were charged off more than seven years ago and should no longer appear on my credit report. I respectfully request that you delete these accounts immediately and forward me an updated report when you've completed the adjustment.

Co Name:

1)

2)

3)

4)

5)

I'll wait 30 days from the date you receive this letter for your response.

Sincerely,

BUREAU NAME   YOUR NAME
ADDRESS   ADDRESS
CITY, ST, ZIP   CITY, ST, ZIP
CUSTOMER REL.   SS#, D.O.B.

To whom it may concern,

The following items appearing on my credit report are being reported incorrectly. These items belong to my former spouse and I was never a signer on any of them.

Therefore, I respectfully request that you investigate and delete these items from my credit report. I would also appreciate the names, addresses, and phone #s of those with whom you checked so I can follow up.

Co Name:

1)

2)

3)

4)

5)

I'll wait 30 days from the date you receive this letter for your response.

Sincerely,

REQUESTING RE-INVESTIGATION FOR SECOND TIME

BUREAU NAME　　　　　　　　　　　YOUR NAME
ADDRESS　　　　　　　　　　　　　　ADDRESS
CITY, ST, ZIP　　　　　　　　　　　　CITY, ST, ZIP
CUSTOMER REL.　　　　　　　　　　SS# D.O.B.

To whom it may concern,

Although I appreciate the removal of some of the items which I disputed in my letter dated _____, I am still in disagreement with the following remaining items which still appear on my report. I noticed that you have marked them "Confirmed by source"; however I find this impossible to accept because I myself could not get those companies to verify these alleged debts to me and I, in theory, am the alleged debtor.

In the interest of fairness, please re-investigate these remaining items and ask for some other verification other than name verification. Any real proof would show these allegations are false and should be deleted.

1)

2)

3)

4)

5)

I would appreciate your response within 30 days considering I have already been greatly hampered by these accounts.

Sincerely,

BANKRUPTCY (DISMISSED OR WITHDRAWN)

BUREAU NAME   YOUR NAME
ADDRESS   ADDRESS
CITY, ST, ZIP   CITY, ST, ZIP
CUSTOMER REL.   SS#, D.O.B.

Customer Relations,

Thank you for removing most of the accounts listed in my letter, dated
_____. Although I appreciate your effort, I am disturbed that you have
maintained the dismissed (filed) bankruptcy and listed it as confirmed. I do
understand that your policy is to keep reporting bankruptcies that are filed,
dismissed, or adjudicated for ten years. However, I recently obtained a copy of the
FCRA and there are no bankruptcies. The law says from the "date of adjudication"
or date of "order for relief" meaning discharge date.

Obviously, if Congress wanted people to be punished for a dismissed case
or the simple filing of one, they would have added it into the law. Fortunately,
they did not and will not because any case, civil or otherwise, which is dismissed
and no longer exists in the eyes of the law and a case filed may have never
actually been adjudicated. Therefore, it certainly is no right of yours to maintain
information in which the government has deemed nonexistent.

In the interest of fairness and in accordance with the FCRA section 605,
please delete this from my profile and send me an updated copy when it has been
corrected. Considering that this does not require an investigation, I would
appreciate your response within two weeks from the date you receive this letter.

Sincerely,

ITEMS BEING REPORTED INACCURATELY

BUREAU NAME   YOUR NAME
ADDRESS   ADDRESS
CITY, ST, ZIP   CITY, ST, ZIP
CUSTOMER REL.   SS#, D.O.B.

To whom it may concern,

The following items listed below are being reported inaccurately. These accounts and events did not occur as reported. i.e., (not late in June, paid, not in BK). I respectfully request that you investigate these accounts and update my credit report to reflect my true credit history.

Co Name:

1)

2)

3)

4)

5)

Additionally, please send me a corrected copy of my report when you've completed the investigation. I'll wait 30 days for your response.

Sincerely,

BUREAU NAME   YOUR NAME
ADDRESS   ADDRESS
CITY, ST, ZIP   CITY, ST, ZIP
CUSTOMER REL.   SS#, D.O.B.

To whom it may concern,

I appreciate your deleting the accounts that were appearing on my credit report incorrectly. However, I am still in strong disagreement with the following remaining items. These accounts are still being reported inaccurately and are extremely injurious to me.

I respectfully request that you re-investigate these remaining items and delete them as the others.

Co. Name:

1)

2)

3)

4)

5)

Additionally, please send me the name, address and phone number of those with whom you verify so I may follow up.

Sincerely,

INQUIRIES NOT AUTHORIZED BY YOU

BUREAU NAME   YOUR NAME
ADDRESS   ADDRESS
CITY, ST, ZIP   CITY, ST, ZIP
CUSTOMER REL.   SS#, D.O.B.

To whom it may concern,

Please delete the following inquiries that are appearing on my credit report. These are prescreening inquiries and were not a genuine offer of credit.

1]
2]
3]
4]
5]

Additionally, I would like the names, addresses, and phone numbers of these companies so that I can follow up.

Sincerely,

VALIDATION OF DEBT TO COLLECTION AGENCY

BUREAU NAME   YOUR NAME
ADDRESS   ADDRESS
CITY, ST, ZIP   CITY, ST, ZIP
CUSTOMER REL.   ACCOUNT #

To whom it may concern,

    Recently your company sent a letter alleging that I owed a debt to _____. This allegation is in error. I would like you to send me the following proofs, assuming they exist in accordance with the FDCPA section 809.

1]

2]

3]

4]

5]

    I will wait 30 days for your response. In addition, I wish not to be contacted by phone again by anyone in your organization at my home or at any other location under any circumstances. From this point forward, all communication will exist through the mail only.

Sincerely,

RESPONSE TO NON-COMPLIANCE

BUREAU NAME   YOUR NAME
ADDRESS   ADDRESS
CITY, ST, ZIP   CITY, ST, ZIP
CUSTOMER REL.   SS#, D.O.B.

To whom it may concern,

Enclosed is a copy of a letter mailed to you on (date) requesting proof of the debt your company alleged I owed. The return receipt is/was signed on (date), copy enclosed. It has since been more than 30 days and I have yet to receive anything from you in the way of proof to validate the debt.

Section 807 of the Fair Debt Collection Practices Act states that any information which is "known to be false, or should be known to be false", cannot be reported to any credit bureau.

Therefore, in accordance with this Act, I respectfully request you remove this from my credit report within 10 days of receipt of this second letter. A copy of everything enclosed has been sent to all three credit bureaus for their review.

Sincerely,

BUREAU NAME   YOUR NAME
ADDRESS   ADDRESS
CITY, ST, ZIP   CITY, ST, ZIP
CUSTOMER REL.   SS#, D.O.B.

To whom it may concern,

Enclosed please find a copy of a letter sent to the following creditors whom you claimed verified the negative accounts on my credit report, requesting proof of those debts in accordance with the law. These letters were sent certified mail return receipt requested (copy enclosed) and there has been no response from the creditor or any other attempt to validate this debt to me.

I find it next to impossible that you claim to have verified this debt with them when they cannot or will not verify to me, even though I am the alleged debtor.

This letter is to notify you that this (these) debt(s) have not been validated in accordance with the law and as I stated in my first request to you (did not belong to me) (was paid on time), etc.

Therefore, I am requesting that you remove this (these) account(s) from my credit report in the next 10 days. I feel this is more than enough time considering it has already been a total of (30, 60, 90) days.

Sincerely,

YOU'RE USING A CREDIT REPAIR SERVICE CLAIM

BUREAU NAME   YOUR NAME
ADDRESS   ADDRESS
CITY, ST, ZIP   CITY, ST, ZIP
CUSTOMER REL.   SS#, D.O.B.

To whom it may concern,

     I am in receipt of your letter dated (date) claiming that you are not obligated to investigate the accounts that I had listed in my letter to you dated (date) sent return receipt requested (copy enclosed), because in your opinion I am using a "credit repair service".

     I find this behavior on your part reprehensible! How dare you deny me my right to have my credit report show a true and accurate accounting of my history on the ridiculous ground that I am using an outside service for help.

     First of all, there is nowhere in the FCRA that states you can make such a claim. However, it does say that I have a right to dispute any item that I do not agree with the "completeness or accuracy". For your information, I got my assistance from the FTC in Washington DC. I have forwarded a copy of this illegal and unconscionable letter of yours to them.

     I expect you to fulfill your obligation under the law and re-investigate my claim within 30 days or less and will not tolerate any further stall tactics on your part.

Sincerely,

THE OLD "FRIVOLOUS AND IRRELEVANT" TRICK

BUREAU NAME   YOUR NAME
ADDRESS   ADDRESS
CITY, ST, ZIP   CITY, ST, ZIP
CUSTOMER REL.   SS#, D.O.B.

To whom it may concern,

"The presence of contradictory information in the consumer files does not in and of itself constitute reasonable grounds for believing the dispute is frivolous and irrelevant".

Yes, I am in receipt of your *illegal* letter dated (_/_/_) claiming that my dispute is "frivolous and irrelevant". Of course, you have no way of knowing that because thus far you have not fulfilled your obligation under the law and investigated my dispute.

How dare you call me a liar, when every newspaper in the country has reported that more than half the files contained in your database are loaded with inaccuracies?

I have forwarded a copy of this *illegal* letter to the FTC Washington DC, and the sub-committee on banking credit and insurance. I fully expect that you will fulfill your legal obligation and investigate the items contained in my letter dated (date) sent to you certified mail return receipt requested. I will follow up with a phone call to confirm when you will begin the work and when it will be completed.

Sincerely,

CREDIT REPORT REQUEST

BUREAU NAME
ADDRESS
CITY, ST, ZIP
CUSTOMER REL.

YOUR NAME
ADDRESS
CITY, ST, ZIP
SS# D.O.B.

Customer Relations,

Please send me a copy of my credit report. I have enclosed copies of my electric bill and my social security card as proof of who I am.

Sincerely,

45

BUREAU NAME   YOUR NAME
ADDRESS   ADDRESS
CITY, ST, ZIP   CITY, ST, ZIP
CUSTOMER REL.   SS#, D.O.B.
DATE

To whom it may concern,

Please remove the following file variations/checkpoints that are appearing on my credit report incorrectly. These obvious typos or errors make my credit report appear as though I'm attempting to commit a fraud.

My correct information is listed on this letter and is the only information that should appear on my report. Please make these adjustments and send me a copy of my updated file for my records.

List all file variations you would like removed.

1]
2]
3]
4]

Additionally, I would appreciate the names, addresses, and phone numbers of the companies who caused these errors so I may follow-up.

Sincerely,

PAYMENTS SHOWING LATE

BUREAU NAME   YOUR NAME
ADDRESS   ADDRESS
CITY, ST, ZIP   CITY, ST, ZIP
CUSTOMER REL.   SS#, D.O.B.
DATE

To whom it may concern,

    The following items listed on my credit report are reflecting late payments. These accounts are showing in error and were (paid on time) (never late as reported). Please re-investigate the accounts mentioned below and update my credit report to reflect my true history.

1]

2]

3]

4]

5]

    I would appreciate your sending me an updated copy of my file when you have completed the investigation.

Sincerely,

STUDENT LOAN DEFAULT & DEFERRMENT

BUREAU NAME   YOUR NAME
ADDRESS   ADDRESS
CITY, ST, ZIP   CITY, ST, ZIP
CUSTOMER REL.   SS#, D.O.B.
DATE

To whom it may concern,

The following student loan(s) are being reported incorrectly on my credit report. These loans were not in default as shown on my report. They were deferred and that is reported correctly in my file. Please remove the default as soon as possible and send me an updated copy of my credit report when you've completed your investigation.

1]

2]

3]

Additionally, I would appreciate the names, addresses, and phone numbers of the individuals with whom you verified so that I may follow up.

Sincerely,

BANKRUPTCY SHOWN FILED IN WRONG LOCATION

BUREAU NAME   YOUR NAME
ADDRESS   ADDRESS
CITY, ST, ZIP   CITY, ST, ZIP
CUSTOMER REL.   SS#, D.O.B.
DATE

To whom it may concern,

    The following bankruptcy listed on my credit report is being listed in error. I never filed a bankruptcy in (city or county) and there is no bankruptcy in my name listed in that Federal bankruptcy court. Please remove this prejudicial notation as soon as possible and send me an updated copy of my report for my records.

*BK – list info with (city or county) notated on your report.

Sincerely,

BUREAU NAME   YOUR NAME
ADDRESS   ADDRESS
CITY, ST, ZIP   CITY, ST, ZIP
CUSTOMER REL.   SS#, D.O.B.
DATE

To whom it may concern,

The following tax liens appearing on my credit report are being listed in error. These liens were never litigated and never led to any kind of adjudication (there is no tax lien listed in the/my name in _____ County, i.e. "two point match"). Please remove these notations from my credit report to reflect my true history.

1)

2)

I spoke to someone in your office who said this was probably a "merged file". I'm not exactly sure what that is but it sounds like a computer error. I would appreciate you correcting this error as soon as possible considering the severity of the implication.

Sincerely,

BUREAU NAME
ADDRESS
CITY, ST, ZIP
CUSTOMER REL.
DATE

YOUR NAME
ADDRESS
CITY, ST, ZIP
SS#, D.O.B.

To whom it may concern,

The below listed item(s) are being reported incorrectly. There never was a car repossession for (x dollars), or (in June of 92) etc., i.e., "late payment strategy". Please re-investigate and delete this information from my credit report. When you're finished, I would appreciate an updated copy for my records.

1)

2)

I would also appreciate the names, addresses, and phone numbers of those with whom you make contact so if necessary I may follow-up.

Sincerely,

Defendant shows that:

A final judgment was entered against defendant in this action on (date).
The final judgment was based on a default entered against this defendant on (date).

After the default and prior to final judgment the record shows that a trial was held before the court. The record shows service of a notice of the trial on defendant by a certificate of service of plaintiff's attorney.

The notice as mailed to (address).

The return of process server shows that service of the process and complaint was made on defendant by serving a person over the age of 15 years at defendant's usual place of abode party the same address and naming the person as (name)

Defendant:
  Defendant never lived at (address)
  Does not know (name)
  (Name) has never resided at defendant's usual place of abode
  Defendant never received original complaint or process alleged to
  have been served
  Defendant did not receive the notice of trial

As a result the judgment is void for lack of jurisdiction over the person of defendant and defendant moves that the judgment and default be vacated

The undersigned certifies that a copy has been mailed to (plaintiff's attorney)

NAME
ADDRESS
CITY, ST, ZIP, PHONE
    DEFENDANT: _____

       PLAINTIFF   IN THE (NAME COURT)

         Vs.

DEFENDANT IN THE CITY OF   (CNTY)

CASE # _____

REVIEWING THE UPDATED CREDIT REPORT

When the **UPDATED** copy of your credit report comes, compare it to the original credit report and verify that everything is being reported correctly. Review the new updated credit report very carefully.

UPDATES TO LOOK FOR	
Account Balances	The total amount of money owned to a third party such as a credit card company, utility company, mortgage holder or other type of lender or creditor.
Account Numbers	The primary identifier for ownership of an account. The account could be a checking or brokerage account, or a loan number.
Late Payments	A payment that has not been made as of its due date.

Every change to your credit report is important in cleaning up your credit and increasing your credit score.

FILE VARIATIONS

File variations errors will trigger one of three notations, **HAWK ALERTS**, **CHECKPOINTS**, and **AKA ALERTS** to appear on your credit report. Here are some samples of file variations errors to double check for when checking the updated credit report

FILE VARIATIONS ERRORS	
Spelling of your Name	Check to make sure the spelling of your name is correct.
Wrong Address	Check to make sure your correct mailing address is being reported.
Wrong SSN	Check to make sure your social security number is being reported correctly.
Typos	Check for misspelled words on your credit report.

CHAPTER 12

A NOTATION APPEARS ON YOUR CREDIT REPORT

When a notation such as **"AKA Alert" or "HAWK Alert"** appears on your credit report, bring this to the bureaus attention. Just write your letter and send it to the bureaus to inform them of the error that is causing an alert to appear on your credit report. Explain what the error is that you want corrected. For example your social security number is incorrect and you would like for it to be corrected.

Once your credit report is clear from adverse information you do not want these alerts on your credit report. Too many of these alerts on your report will make it look like you are up to an unlawful act.

It is important to remember that if these are not removed from your credit report they can cause a great deal of problems when applying for credit. Remember a merged report of someone with a similar name or a typo could cause you aggravation when it comes to your credit report.

After completing the process of cleaning up your credit report next is the task of managing your credit report.

Begin managing your credit report by requesting a copy of your report once or twice a year to check for damaging or potentially damaging notations.

LAST TRANSACTION

On your credit reports you will see dates that appear for individual accounts that have a "date of last activity or transaction". This account remains on your credit report for seven years. The bureaus use this as a way of determining when the account should come off a person's credit report. However, the Fair Credit Reporting Act makes no mention of a "last activity date" to be used as a point of reference to determine for an account to remain on an individual's credit report.

ACTIVITY DATE

Remember when checking your credit report to see if the information is being reported correctly or incorrectly, check the activity date the credit bureaus have in your credit file.

WHAT THE LAW DOES SAY IS THIS

Adverse information will remain in a credit file for seven years from the "date charged off to profit and loss" or the "date of adjudication".

CHAPTER 13

HOW TO IMPROVE YOUR CREDIT SCORE

Because each borrower's credit score is a reflection of his or her unique credit profile, it is not possible to quantify in advance exactly how each item in your credit history numerically impacts upon your ultimate credit score. No one can tell you, for example, how much your credit score will be affected if you pay off a delinquent account or cancel a credit card. What is known, however, is that there are things you can do to improve your credit profile.

MAKING TIMELY PAYMENTS

Making your payments on time is the best way to increase your score. Delinquencies, foreclosures, bankruptcies and judgments will decrease your score.

AVOID DELINQUENT CREDIT OBLIGATIONS

Occasionally consumers will miss a payment on one of their bills like a car loan, merchant account, credit card, or car loan. It can happen for a number of reasons. Avoid situations like these because they will have an effect on your credit score.

Lenders take into consideration an establish pattern of how an individual pays their bills and manage their debt to determine the risk factor before funding a loan. If you have established a pattern of paying your bills on time the credit risk factor is not as great as an individual that has establish a pattern of being late on their payments. A lender will be very reluctant, even unwilling to extend credit to a consumer that establishes a pattern of mismanaging their debt. Remember, mismanaging your debt will be reflected on your credit report and will affect your credit score as a result of it.

Your credit score will also be affected if you have a bankruptcy, repossession, or a foreclosure on a mortgage showing on your credit report. These situations will have an effect on your ability to apply for credit in the future also.

THE NUMBER OF TRADE LINES

The number of credit cards, lines of credit, and other types of credit / Trade Lines you have available will affect your score. If you have a lot of trade lines, this may decrease your score because of the risk that you might not be able to pay off all of your accounts, and this may affect your ability to pay off your mortgage loan. You may wish to consider canceling credit cards you do not use regularly or choosing (2) or (4) cards to use and canceling the rest. If you close or cancel an account voluntarily it will not have a negative effect on your credit score. You may wish to reconsider accepting "Pre-approved" offers for credit cards, or if you accept an offer, perhaps you should cancel another credit card. On the other hand, if you have no trade lines, this will likely decrease your score. Lenders generally want to see that you have some available credit and that you can handle your credit wisely.

AVOID UNNECESSARILY HIGH CREDIT LIMITS

Paying your bills on time is important, but controlling how much money you owe on credit card and other debts are also just as important. A lender will show considerable concern about the credit risk of a consumer who overextends themselves by the use of their available credit.

Lenders also consider the amount of credit available (your credit limit) compared to your income when making underwriting decisions. Having credit limits that are too high (relative to your income) can affect your score just like having too many trade lines.

CHAPTER 14

WHY THE LENDER IS CONCERNED

You might be asking yourself, why would a lender be concerned if you are making your payments on time? Paying your bills on time or not paying your bills on time starts and ends with YOU!

Many consumers today have credit cards and have used them to their maximum, creating financial difficulty for themselves to make the monthly payments. Consumers who find themselves in this situation also find that the ability to make the monthly payments becomes a challenge and overwhelming. They will ignore the debt hoping that it will go away or simply stop making the payment on the debt altogether.

Things may appear to be fine as long as you are making your monthly payments on time. In reality you are at a higher credit risk than those consumers that manage their credit debt more conservatively.

Your credit score is based on how millions of consumers manage their credit debt. This allows the scoring process to identify consumers that are overextended or are becoming delinquent in making the payment on their credit debt reflected in a lower credit score.

HOW YOU USE CREDIT

The amount outstanding on each of your credit cards will also affect your score. In general, the lower the amount outstanding, the more likely it is that your score will be higher.

DO NOT APPLY FOR CREDIT YOU DO NOT NEED

Whenever you apply for credit, the creditor will obtain a credit report from one or more of the three credit report bureaus. Each such credit inquiry will stay on your record and will affect your credit score. Even if you are turned down for the credit or change your mind and withdraw your application, your credit score will be affected. This is because each inquiry suggests that you are increasing the amount of credit available to you. Because Social Security numbers are used to run a credit report, make certain you know how they are going to use it before you give your Social Security number to someone. The credit report bureaus generally consider all inquiries received within a 14 day period as 1 inquiry so the additional inquiries will not affect your credit score.

CHAPTER 15

HOW TO PUT A FRAUD ALERT ON YOUR CREDIT FILE

On January1, 2003 a new law went into effect for California residents allowing you to place a freeze on your credit report. This new law is called the California SB168 freeze law.

This new California bill SB 168 tightens access to your credit data even more by allowing you to freeze all access to your credit file.
Putting a fraud alert on your credit file is one of the first things you should do if you suspect someone is trying to open credit accounts in your name.

A fraud alert can be, and sometimes is ignored by creditors. If you suspect you are a victim of identity theft or have already become a victim, fraud alerts are only a start in trying to protect your credit. You also need to pay close attention to your credit report to make sure no new credit inquiries or credit accounts are being opened.

WHAT IS A FRAUD ALERT?

A fraud alert is something that the major credit bureaus attach to your credit report. When someone tries to open up a credit account by getting a new credit card, mortgage loan, cell phone, in your name etc., the lender should contact you by phone to verify that you really want to open a new account.

HOW TO SET UP A FRAUD ALERT?

It's pretty easy. Just contact the fraud department of each of the credit bureaus and ask them to flag your credit file for fraud.

WHAT HAPPENS WHEN A FRAUD ALERT IS ACTIVATED?

Within 24 hours, an alert will be placed on your credit file at all three major credit bureaus. Your name will be removed from all pre-approved credit and insurance offers for two years. The fraud alert will remain in place for 3 months (Experian), 6 months (Equifax), 12 months (Trans Union). When the time runs out, you'll need to reactivate the alert. You can also apply for a 7-year victim statement that will keep the alert in place for you. For this, you will have to provide proof that you have been a victim of fraud.

WHAT ARE THE DRAWBACKS OF A FRAUD ALERT?

With a fraud alert active, you have to be available at either your work phone, home phone, cell phone or mobile device to approve opening a credit account.

CHAPTER 16

HOW TO FREEZE YOUR CREDIT FILES

Consumers, who live in California, have the right to put a "security freeze" on their credit file. A security freeze means that your file cannot be shared with potential creditors. A security freeze can help prevent identity theft. If your credit files were frozen, even someone who has your name and Social Security number would probably not be able to get credit in your name.
A security freeze is free to identity theft victims who have a police report of identity theft, or a DMV investigative report of identity theft.
If you are not an identity theft victim, it will cost you a fee of $10 to place a security freeze with each of the credit reporting bureaus or a total cost of $30 to freeze your files. For adults 65 and older the cost is free.
When placing a freeze on your account you will need to provide the following information to the different agencies.

Equifax Security Freeze, P.O. Box 105788 Atlanta, GA 30348

- Send by certified mail
- Name, current and former address, Social Security number, date of birth
- Pay by check, money order, or credit card

Experian Security Freeze, P. O. Box 9554 Allen, TX 75013

- Send by certified mail
- Full name, with middle initial and Jr. / Sr.
- Current address and home addresses for past five years, Social Security number, birth date, two proofs of residence (copy of driver's license, utility bill, insurance statement, bank statement)
- Pay by check, money order or credit card.

**TransUnion Fraud Victim Assistance,
P. O. Box 6790 Fullerton, CA 92834-6790**

- Send by regular or certified mail
- First name, middle initial, last name, Jr.
- Current home address and addresses for past five years, Social Security number, birth date
- Pay by check, money order or credit card.

CAN I OPEN NEW CREDIT ACCOUNTS IF MY FILES ARE FROZEN?

YES! If you want to open a new credit account or get a new loan, you can lift the freeze on your credit file. You can lift it for a period of time, or you can lift it for a specific creditor. After you send your letter asking for the freeze, each of the credit bureaus will send you a Personal Identification Number (PIN). You will also get instructions on how to lift the freeze. You can lift the freeze by phone, using your PIN. The credit bureaus must lift your freeze within three days. In many states it will cost $10 per credit reporting agency each time you lift the freeze.

FRAUD ALERT VS A FREEZE ON YOUR CREDIT REPORT

A fraud alert is a special message on the report that a credit issuer receives when checking a consumer credit rating. It tells the credit issuer that there may be fraud involved in the account. Fraud alerts can help protect you against identity theft, but a fraud alert can also slow down your ability to get new credit. It should not stop you from using your existing credit cards or other accounts. A security freeze means that your credit file cannot be shared with potential creditors, insurance companies or employers doing background checks. Most businesses will not open credit accounts without checking a consumer credit history first.

SECURITY FREEZE PROCESSES AND ACTIVITY REQUEST	
Request for place freeze on credit report.	Takes (5) five business days after receiving your request for a freeze to be placed on your credit report.
Request to remove security freeze.	Takes (3) three business days after receiving your request for a freeze to be removed from your credit report.
What information is displayed when a request is made?	A creditor will see a message or a code indicating that the file is frozen.
Can I request a copy of my credit report if my account is frozen?	Yes! You can request a copy of your report if your files are frozen.

CAN ANYONE SEE MY CREDIT FILE IF IT IS FROZEN?

When you have a security freeze on your credit file, certain entities still have access to it. Your report can still be released to your existing creditors or to collection agencies acting on their behalf. They can use it to review or collect on your account. Other creditors may also use your information to make offers of credit, unless you opt out of receiving such offers. See below for how to opt out of pre-approved credit offers. Government agencies may have access for collecting child support payments or taxes or for investigating Medical fraud. Government agencies may also have access in response to a court or administrative order, a subpoena, or a search warrant.

DO I HAVE TO FREEZE MY FILE WITH ALL THREE CREDIT BUREAUS?

Yes. Different credit issuers may use different credit bureaus. If you want to stop your credit file from being viewed, you need to freeze it with Equifax, Experian and Trans Union.

WILL A FREEZE LOWER MY CREDIT SCORE?

No! A freeze on your report will not lower your credit score.

CAN EMPLOYERS DO A BACKGROUND CHECK IF I HAVE A FREEZE ON MY CREDIT FILE?

No. You would have to lift the freeze to allow a background check or to apply for insurance, just as you would to apply for credit. The process for lifting the freeze is described above.

DOES FREEZING MY FILE MEAN THAT I WON'T RECEIVE PRE-APPROVE CREDIT OFFERS?

No! You can stop the pre-approved credit offers by calling, 1-888-5OPTOUT - (1-888-567-8688). Or you can do this online at www.optoutprescreen.com. This will stop most of the offers like the ones that go through the credit bureaus. It's good for five years or you can make it permanent.

DOES MY SPOUSE'S FILE HAVE TO BE FROZEN TOO?

Yes! Both spouses have to freeze their separate credit files, via separate letters requesting the freeze, in order to get the benefit. That means the total cost for freezing is: ($10 x 3 credit bureaus) x (2 people) = $60.

ASSEMBLY BILL NUMBER - 2374 CHAPTER 645

An act to amend Sections 1785.11.2 and 1785.15 of the Civil Code, relating to consumer credit reports bill, was approved on September 27, 2012, Filed Secretary of State September 27, 2012.
If you are 65 years of age or older you will pay a fee of no more than $5 for placing, lifting, or removing a security freeze.

CHAPTER 17

PROTECTING YOUR INFORMATION FROM IDENTITY THEFT

IDENTITY THEFT PREVENTION

An identity thief takes some piece of your personal information and uses it without your knowledge. The thief may run up debts or even commit crimes in your name. The following tips can help you lower your risk of becoming a victim.

PROTECT YOUR SOCIAL SECURITY NUMBER

Don't carry your Social Security card in your wallet. If your health plan (other than Medicare) or another card uses your Social Security number, you should ask the company for a different number that can be used in place of your SSN.

FIGHT "PHISHING"- DON'T TAKE THE BAIT

Scam artists use "**Phishing**" to look for victims by pretending to be banks, a store or government agencies. They do this over the phone, in e-mails and in the regular mail. Don't give out your personal information - unless you made the contact. Don't respond to a request to verify your account number or password. Legitimate companies will not request this kind of information in this way.

KEEP YOUR IDENTITY FROM GETTING TRASHED

Shred or tear up papers with personal information before you throw them away. Shred credit card offers and "convenience checks" that you don't use.

PROTECT YOUR PERSONAL FINANCIAL INFORMATION

California law requires your bank and other financial services companies to get your permission before sharing your personal information.

SHIELD YOUR COMPUTER FROM VIRUSES AND SPIES.

Protect your personal information on your home computer. Use strong passwords with at least eight characters, including a combination of letters, numbers, and symbols, easy for you to remember, but difficult for others to guess. Use firewall and virus protection software that you update regularly. Steer clear of spyware and download free software only from sites you know and trust. Don't install software without knowing what it is and don't click on links in pop-up windows or in spam e-mail.

CLICK WITH CAUTION

When shopping online, check out a Web site before entering your credit card number or other personal information. Read the privacy policy and look for opportunities to opt out of information sharing. (If there is no privacy policy posted, shop elsewhere). Only enter personal information on secure Web pages with "https" in the address bar and a padlock symbol at the bottom of the browser window. These are signs that your information will be encrypted or scrambled, protecting it from hackers.

CHECK YOUR BILLS AND BANK STATEMENTS

Open your credit card bills and bank statements right away. Check carefully for any unauthorized charges or withdrawals and report them immediately. Call if bills don't arrive on time. It may mean that someone has changed contact information to hide fraudulent charges.

STOP PRE-APPROVED CREDIT OFFERS

Stop most pre-approved credit card offers. They make a tempting target for identity thieves who steal your mail. Have your name removed from credit bureau marketing lists. Call toll-free 888-5OPTOUT (888-567-8688).

ASK QUESTIONS

Ask questions whenever you are asked for personal information that seems inappropriate for the transaction. Ask how the information will be used and if it will be shared. Ask how it will be protected. Explain that you're concerned about identity theft. If you're not satisfied with the answers, consider going somewhere else.

CHECK YOUR CREDIT REPORTS - FOR FREE.

One of the best ways to protect you from identity theft is to monitor your credit history. You can get one free credit report every year from each of the three national credit bureaus: Equifax, Experian and Trans Union. Request all three reports at once, or be your own no-cost credit-monitoring service. Just spread out your requests, ordering from a different bureau every four months. Comprehensive monitoring services from the credit bureaus will cost from $44 to over $100 per year.).

MANAGE YOUR CREDIT REORT

It is very important to remember that your credit is a form of currency. With identity theft on the rise, you must take the position of managing your credit like your bank account. Obtain a copy of your credit report by sending certified letters to the three major credit-reporting bureaus. Or go online to request a copy of your credit report. Remember to include your name, your address, and your date of birth, a copy of your social security card and a copy of your electric bill.

CHAPTER 18

DEBT MANAGEMENT
TIPS ON HOW TO GET OUT OF DEBT

CREDIT CARD DEBT FREEDOM

Cut in half any credit cards that you have maxed out.

If you are using retail cards like gas cards or department store cards, stop using them and cut them up too. The goal here is to use only one credit card to make purchases for the things that can be paid off in a short period of time to help with getting you're spending under control. If you need to make an emergency purchase, use the one credit card to make that purchase.

TRANSFER YOUR BALANCE TO A LOW-RATE CARD

Transferring one credit card balance to a promotional credit card with a zero percent offer can be a good option if you plan to pay off your balance completely. Remember you will be charged a transfer fee.

NEGOTIATE A LOWER RATE

You can negotiate a lower rate if you have a good to excellent credit score.

CLOSE UNUSED CREDIT CARDS

Remember if you have credit cards that you are no longer using or have never used, you should close those credit card accounts and shred the credit cards. Using a shredder is recommended for destroying junk mail, sensitive documents and credit cards that you no longer are using.

MONITOR AND MANAGE YOUR CREDIT CARD UTILIZATION

Credit utilization is calculated by creditors, and measures how much your credit card limits are to your credit card balance. In fact your credit utilization makes up 30% of your FICO score. Other factors that influence your credit score in addition to your credit utilization are: Payment history (35%), how old is the credit or the age of the credit (15%), your mix of credit (10%) and the number of inquires on your credit report makes up the remaining (10%) of your FICO score.

If you have a credit card with a credit limit of $1,000 and you buy something for $300 that puts your credit utilization at 30%. To understand more on how this works simply divide the balance of your credit card by the limit of the credit card and multiply that number by 100.

Credit Utilization Calculation
(Credit card balance) ÷ (limit of credit card) x (100) = (Credit utilization)

The number you come up with is very important because you want to keep your credit utilization low. This shows the creditor that only small amounts of the credit they loaned to you is being used.

You should try and always have a low credit card balance; this will ensure that your credit utilization will remain low.

Your credit report is a snapshot in time of your credit history of what a creditor that has loaned you credit is reporting to the credit bureaus. Creditors report your credit activity to the bureaus at different times affecting your credit utilization number. Paying off the balance on a credit card in full to get a zero "0" balance. Will lower your credit utilization and improve your FICO score. This will not show up on your credit report if the creditor reports to the bureaus a different balance before you paid the balance off in full.

CHAPTER 19

COMMUNICATE WITH ALL OF YOUR LENDERS

Paying your bills on time is a great way to maintain good credit and stay out of debt. But if you find that you are not financially able to pay your bills on time, don't hide from lenders or ignore creditors when they call or send you letters. Contact them and talk to them about how you can work out a payment plan to fit your budget. You want to work with the creditors before they send your account to their collection department or a third party collection agency. Paying something towards your bills is better than not paying anything at all and over time paying your bills will become more manageable to the point where you can pay them off.

MANAGE YOUR BILLS

Managing your finances starts with knowing how much money you have available. Make sure you are spending your money in the right places. A good way to help with managing your money is to use a bill pay system. Using a bill pay system will help you to organize and make bill management easy and without the stress that comes with paying bills. Paying your bills online is a great way to take advantage of a bill pay system. They provide you with access to your accounts so you can view your statements and bills online. Your account can be set up to send out an alert via email to let you know when your next payment is due. Using a good bill management system will help you manage your bills, expenses and maintain a monthly budget.

CUT SPENDING

When setting up your budget, ask yourself, if you need all the things that you are spending your money on. What can you cut back on or eliminate to reduce spending? The best way to answer these questions is to create a list of what you are spending your money on. Using the bill pay system of your choice will help you to identify the areas where you can cut your spending. Once you have your budget in place you must be disciplined and stick to the budget plan. Every dollar counts, so learn to control your impulse buying.

METHODS OF PAYING OFF YOUR CREDIT CARDS

PAYING OFF HIGHEST-INTEREST VS. LOWEST BALANCE

The bills with the highest interest rates should be paid off first.
After you have paid off the bills with the highest interest rates, start focusing on paying off the next bill with the highest interest rate. You will find by paying off the high-interest first, it will get rid of maintenance fees and save you money in the long run. You should also know that if the card that you are paying off has the highest interest rate and a high balance, it will take longer to pay that card off.

LOWEST BALANCE PAY OFF OPTION

If paying off a card with a high-interest and a high balance will burden you financially, focus on paying off the bills with a lower balance first to chip away at your debt. This will give you more money to pay towards the larger bills with the high interest rate. Remember paying off your debt is an investment in you and it puts money back in your pocket.

USE CASH WHENEVER POSSIBLE

Paying for items with actual dollars from your wallet will make you think twice about creating new debt. Every dollar counts when it comes to knowing how much money you have on hand.

ADD ADDITIONAL INCOME

- If your belt cannot get any tighter and spending less is not helping much, find a way to make more money. Now is the time to look for a part-time or freelance job.

- Look around your house and make a list of things of value that you no longer use, want, or need that can be sold to add more income to your budget. Remember there are hidden riches in those things that you no longer have a need for or are using.

- Also, remove any emotions to items that you want to sell when it comes to making money to add to your budget to pay your bills. Bills don't wait. They just keep coming in the mail, knocking at your financial door, and add up to a mountain of debt if they go unpaid.

- Be creative when adding additional income to your bottom line.

CHAPTER 20

GET OUT OF DEBT AND STAY ON TRACK

Once you have your system and your budget in place and a plan to help keep your eye on the prize of being debt free, continue to pay down your debt one payment at a time. Do not allow yourself to become distracted by choosing to purchase unnecessary items and control impulse buying. If your friend or neighbor goes out and buys a new car, or is making incredible upgrades to his/her house, it does not mean that you should go out and spend money that you can use to pay down your debt. If you do, you will lose your focus of your desired goal to get out of debt.

If you find that you are eating out more than you are at home, cut back and start cooking meals at home. If you have a gym membership that you are not using, cancel it and put the money back in your pocket to pay down your debt.

Paying down debt is not easy and it will take hard work and time on your part. It will be difficult to pass up a good deal, or not to buy the next new toy on the market, but you will have to buckle down and stick to your goal of paying down your debt. Remember every payment that you make towards paying down your debt is an investment for a better future.

Putting off making purchases that you do not need until you get rid of your debt, will let you know what you can live with and live without.

Remember the goal is to pay down your debt and get out of the debt cycle. No one likes being a prisoner to debt.

You can achieve the goal of getting out of debt also by changing your thought process about spending, saving, and debt. It's your money and it's your debt so changing how you think about how you spend your money is a good step towards having the will power to focus on paying down your debt.

Elimination of debt will give you the freedom of building a better future for you and your family.

WHO OWES YOU MONEY

DEBTORS:

If you have loaned money out and have not been paid back, write down who owes you money and attempt to collect. You are working to get out of debt and every amount of money helps. Also, having them pay back the debt to you helps them to get out of debt and on to the path of debt freedom.

NAME:_____

ADDRESS:_____

NAME:_____

ADDRESS:_____

NAME:_____

ADDRESS:_____

NAME:_____

ADDRESS:_____

NAME: _____

ADDRESS: _____

NAME: _____

ADDRESS: _____

WHO DO YOU OWE MONEY TO

CREDITORS:

Write down who you owe money to. Include car loans, student loans, bank loans, credit cards do not overlook any persons or firms that you owe money to. Making a list by writing the names down helps by staying focused on paying your debt down and having real financial freedom.

NAME:_____

ADDRESS:_____

NAME:_____

ADDRESS:_____

NAME:_____

ADDRESS:_____

NAME:_____

ADDRESS:_____

NAME: _____

ADDRESS: _____

NAME: _____

ADDRESS: _____

BIBLIOGRAPHY

Assembly Bill No. 2374 Chapter 645 an Act to amend Sections 1785.11.2 and 1785.15 of the Civil Code, relating to consumer credit reports.

Fair Credit Reporting Act (FCRA), 15 U.S.C. § 1681 et seq.

Federal Deposit Insurance Corporation (FDIC)

FICO, myFICO, Score Watch, The score lenders use, and The Score That Matters are trademarks or registered trademarks of Fair Isaac Corporation

Equifax and the Equifax marks used herein are registered trademarks of Equifax, Inc

Experian and the Experian marks are trademarks or registered trademarks of Experian Information Solutions, Inc.

OptOutPrescreen.com a centralized service to accept and process requests from consumers to "Opt-In" or "Opt-Out" of firm offers of credit or insurance.

Senate Bill No. 168, Chapter 720, An act to amend Section 1785.15 of, to add Sections 1785.11.1, 1785.11.2, 1785.11.3, 1785.11.4, and 1785.11.6 to, and to add Title 1.81.1 (commencing with Section 1798.85) to Part 4 of Division 3 of, the Civil Code, relating to personal information.

The Bankruptcy Abuse Prevention and Consumer Protection Act of 2005 (BAPCPA)

The Federal Trade Commission (FTC) is the nation's consumer protection agency. The FTC works to prevent fraudulent, deceptive and unfair business practices in the marketplace.

TransUnion is a registered trademark of TransUnion.

United States Postal Service (Domestic Mail Only)

INDEX

T

Tax liens, 22
Terms, 31
Trade Lines, 65
Trans Union, 19

U

United States Postal service, 35
unpaid tax liens, 22
unsecured creditor, 32

V

valuable, 16
virus, 74

W

worthiness, 15
written consent, 21
wrong Address, 62
wrong social security number, 62

ABOUT THE AUTHOR

Sherman Fowler has been working with credit challenged clients for over fifteen years. He provides credit educational services and has a passion for helping people clean up their credit and improve their credit score. His educational background in Project Management, The Mortgage Industry, and Real Estate has given him a broad base from which to approach many topics.

Sherman was instrumental in the development of automated underwriting systems and creating training classes for broker training on re-issued reports, merging of conflicting data, and rapid corrections. He is a Realtor, and a member of the California Association of Realtors and the National Association of Realtors, and a member of the Project Management Institute-PMI.

www.ingramcontent.com/pod-product-compliance
Lightning Source LLC
Chambersburg PA
CBHW071454070426
42452CB00039B/1355